# Endorsements

Masey is authentic, open, and truly loves Jesus. Your daughters will definitely be encouraged and strengthened in their walks with the Lord through this devotional as ours have been!

—Jeremy and Adrienne Camp
Contemporary Christian musicians

The beyond-her-years wisdom that pours from Masey's heart, along with her cute sense of humor and raw honesty, will pull you in and make you feel like you're having coffee with a friend.

—Meredith Andrews
Contemporary Christian music artist and songwriter

*It's Worth It* offers day-by-day transparent, relevant, and honest devotions for those seeking purpose on their life journey.

—Hannah Brencher
Author of *If You Find This Letter*, and founder,
The World Needs More Love Letters

The joy of Masey's life in Christ will bring joy into your life too as you read the pages of her book.

—Roger Glidewell
President and founder, Global Youth Ministry

Masey has an exceptional heart for God and a desire to see others know and grow in Christ. Her honesty in these devotions will hit home with anyone who desires to know God more intimately.

—Billy Beacham
Student Discipleship Ministries and See You at the Pole

Young people and adults alike will be challenged and moved through Masey's words of encouragement and hope as they read *It's Worth It*.

—Josh McDowell
Author of 147 books, including *New Evidence That Demands a Verdict* and *More Than a Carpenter*

I couldn't be more grateful or thankful and pleased with how Rachel was portrayed through Masey. You will receive encouragement and inspiration through this wonderful twenty-one-day journey.

—Beth Nimmo
Mother of Rachel Joy Scott

Thank you, Masey, for standing up and coming alongside students with such a strong, impactful message.

—Jay Strack
President, Student Leadership University

I know that Masey's thoughtful reflections and application will encourage all who go through this twenty-one-day encounter.

—Daryl Nuss
National Network of Youth Ministries

When you meet Masey, you can't help but smile. It is obvious Jesus lives in her.

—Mark Roberts
Vice president, First Priority of America

Young and old alike who read this book will say, "It was worth it."

—Greg Davis
President, First Priority of Alabama, and host of "Priority Talk Radio"

21-DAY
DEVOTIONAL

# It's Worth It

### Masey McLain

**BroadStreet**
PUBLISHING

BroadStreet Publishing Group, LLC
Racine, Wisconsin, USA
BroadStreetPublishing.com

In partnership with EndeavorResources.org

It's Worth It: 21-DAY DEVOTIONAL

ISBN-13: 978-1-4245-5442-3 (softcover)
ISBN-13: 978-1-4245-5443-0 (e-book)

Stock or custom editions of BroadStreet Publishing titles may be purchased in bulk for educational, business, ministry, fundraising, or sales promotional use. For information, please e-mail info@broadstreetpublishing.com.

Cover design by Chris Garborg at garborgdesign.com
Typesetting by Katherine Lloyd at theDESKonline.com

Printed in the United States of America
17 18 19 20 21 5 4 3 2 1

# Contents

# Don't Settle

My name is Masey McLain, and I'm an actress who had the incredible opportunity to portray Rachel Scott in the film *I'm Not Ashamed*. Throughout my journey the Lord has taught me a lot about what it means to truly follow him. Honestly, he's still teaching me. Every day.

I wrote these twenty-one daily thoughts because I believe the message of *purpose* is too great to miss out on. You are a unique creation of God, designed to make an impact on the world, to be a force for the kingdom of God. I want to help you discover how to fully live in your calling. In this devotional, I've drawn from my own personal experiences as well as the heart-wrenching process God allowed me to experience while filming *I'm Not Ashamed*.

Sometimes it's not so easy to know or live in your purpose. Life is hard. Things get foggy, truth gets blurred, and the lists of distractions never end. I don't know about you, but I don't want to miss out on what God created me for. I don't want to settle for "just getting by." I want to make a difference.

My prayer is that this devotional will encourage, strengthen, and spur you on in your own journey of following Jesus. I hope you can relate to some of my experiences. More than anything I hope you find yourself wanting to know God more and to live in the fullness of life he has for you. I know that some of the things in here are really simple, maybe a bit "back to the basics." But I believe those things are the most crucial, and we tend to forget them the most.

I remember one day when we were headed to the set of *I'm Not Ashamed.* Executive producer, Benny Proffitt, said, "Y'know, if Rachel could tell us just one thing from heaven, standing in the presence of Jesus and experiencing the glory of God, I believe the one thing she would say is, 'It's worth it.'" I believe that too.

# What I Admire Most

When I played the role of Rachel in *I'm Not Ashamed*, I was asked if I ever felt as if I were having an identity crisis or losing myself by stepping into her shoes. I usually don't get that question when I play a role, but because this time I was portraying a real person, maybe that's why it came up. Throughout filming, everyone (even off set) accidentally called me "Rachel" all the time! I didn't mind it in the least. But the answer to this question was, actually, no. I never once felt I had I lost my own identity while "becoming" Rachel. I think a lot of that is because of how I was able to relate to her while portraying her. To help me do the part, I found that the Lord used experiences in my life I never dreamed he would use. I have come to believe that certain things have happened in my life in order for me to have been able to portray Rachel.

## It's Worth It

When I first heard I was in the running for the part, I had a different view of Rachel than who I found her to be after reading her journals. In my mind, she was perfect. She was a martyr for Christ and did everything right. Who can live up to that?

But that was far from the truth. In reality, she was just like you and me. She was completely human and had weaknesses just like everyone else. The reason her life has made such an impact is because of her relentless pursuit of God. Even though she was not perfect by any means, she chased after the *heart* of God. And you and I have the same opportunity to seek after him: "You will seek me and find me when you seek me with all your heart" (Jeremiah 29:13).

If you want to know God more deeply; experience his intimacy, presence, and abundance; and live fully in your purpose, you must *seek* him with your *whole* heart:

> The LORD has looked down from heaven upon the sons of men to see if there are any who understand, who seek after God. (Psalm 14:2 NASB)

> You, God, are my God, earnestly I seek you; I thirst for you, my whole being longs for you, in a dry and parched land where there is no water. (Psalm 63:1)

> Blessed are those who keep his testimonies, who seek him with their whole heart. (Psalm 119:2 ESV)

## Day 1: What I Admire Most

Rachel did this. Yeah, she messed up; she was confused at times, and she was just trying to figure it all out like all of us. But she decided to seek God's heart above it all, no matter what it looked like or what it cost her. And God did extraordinary things in and through her.

My favorite thing about Rachel was that she counted everything else as loss in view of knowing Jesus. She found that following him was the only thing that satisfied her soul and that was worth surrendering her entire life to.

She understood her purpose. That's what I admire most about Rachel.

I want to have a heart like that. I want to love people with a heart of compassion and see and love people as Jesus does. That's what Rachel desired. And the more she sought the heart of God, the more he changed her heart to look like his.

The most purpose-filled life comes from the deep intimacy of truly knowing God. Rachel didn't wake up one day being kind and compassionate and ready to love people and change the world. I believe all of that was an overflow of her time spent seeking to know his heart.

For all of us, that's our first step in living with purpose. Seek to know God deeply and intimately, the way you know your best friend. As you get to know him, he'll show you what sort of a life he's been dreaming for you and the way to live it.

Day 1 Challenge

Do you want to change the world and make an impact? Seek him with everything you have. Today—can you decide to do that? You don't know if you have tomorrow, but you can decide to live in your purpose today.

If you want to experience more of God, write out a prayer expressing that—nothing fancy. It doesn't have to be complicated. There's no right way or big words you have to use. Just tell him your heart—and ask to know more of his. Throughout the rest of this devotional, I'll start you out with a prayer, and you can take it from there:

*Lord, I want to live in the purpose that you created me for. I want to know you more deeply and experience all that you want me to. Help me to love people the way that you love me.*

# It Won't Make Sense Yet

If you've ever seen the film *Inception,* I'm sure that you, like me, thought it was absolutely brilliant but completely confusing, until the very end. And even then, you probably had to watch it at least three more times to fully understand everything that was going on. Throughout the movie, I'm sure you were constantly asking the person next to you, "What's happening? Did I miss something? *I don't understand! Someone explain!*" (all while stuffing popcorn in your face because it was the only thing that really seemed to make sense). Once the movie ended and all the pieces finally connected, all you could do was sit there, mind blown (and if you're like me, think about it for at least four days after).

Sometimes life seems like that movie. Crazy, unexpected, nonsensical, painful, boring, and exciting scenes are all happening for the sake of the story. Your favorite movie probably takes you on an emotional roller coaster ride. Sometimes you get excited; sometimes you cry. (If you watch a sad movie with me—expect weeping.) There are parts that keep you on the edge of your seat in suspense, and of course parts you want to skip because they're so boring.

We all have our own stories, each made up of different scenes and all ultimately glorifying the Author in their own unique ways.

God is so creative! *Inception* was thought up by brilliant humans. But our personal stories have been thought up by the Creator of the universe. Even more cool to think about: as he creates our stories, God doesn't mess up.

In the scenes that don't make sense, he knows exactly what's going on: "'For My thoughts are not your thoughts, nor are your ways My ways,' declares the LORD. 'For as the heavens are higher than the earth, so are My ways higher than your ways, and My thoughts than your thoughts'" (Isaiah 55:8–9 NASB).

In the scenes that keep us on the edge of our seats, he's doing immeasurably more: "Now to him who is able to do far more abundantly than all that we ask or think, according to the power at work within us, to him be glory in the church and in Christ Jesus throughout all generations, forever and ever. Amen" (Ephesians 3:20–21 ESV).

In the scenes where we are bored out of our minds? He knows they're necessary to the plot: "I wait for the LORD, my soul waits, and in his word I hope" (Psalm 130:5 ESV).

And in the scenes where we can't stop crying, he never leaves us and is the hope that we can cling to: "Praise be to the God and Father of our Lord Jesus Christ, the Father of compassion and the God of all comfort, who comforts us in all our troubles, so that we can comfort those in any trouble with the comfort we ourselves receive from God" (2 Corinthians 1:3–4).

So what keeps us going throughout our stories? A few weeks ago in an acting class, my teacher said something I think will stick with me forever in a really special way. He said, "When you are in an audition, a director is looking for your ability to do something crucial—to live through the scene and to *stay connected* with your scene partner. The goal is to surrender yourself completely to the scene and connect with the other person. Don't lose that connection, no matter what obstacles may come up in the scene. That is where your best work will come from."

How true is this for the believer following Jesus! Our lives have so many different scenes with so many obstacles. Our goal is not to get the lines right or to impress everyone. The goal is not to do it perfectly. The goal is to *stay connected*, no matter what. No matter what comes in the highs and lows of life, the goal is to keep our eyes on Jesus and stay connected with him.

Your story is unique. It's exciting. It's unexpected. It's unnerving. It's full of twists and turns. It's such a beautiful story that you will often look back on it in absolute wonder at what the Lord has been doing. It doesn't have to make sense now. Just stay connected.

It's so easy to get stuck in your circumstances and what's going on around you. Remember—this season won't last forever. This scene will end, and another one will play. Fix your eyes on Jesus throughout whatever part of your story you find yourself in today. He wants to take you to deeper levels of knowing him throughout every "scene" in your life. Wherever you find yourself today, I challenge you to refocus your heart and your mind on Jesus, trusting him as the author of your story. If life doesn't make sense right now or you're lost in trying to figure out what God's doing—that's OK. Just stay connected.

*God, sometimes life gets confusing. Sometimes it just doesn't make sense, and sometimes it's painful. Help me to trust you in the scene I'm in right now. Help me to remember you're in control and show me how to keep my eyes on you.*

Journal

## Day 3

# The Pressure's Off

*If I can be good enough and make the right choices, God will be happy with me.*

Have you ever had this thought? Have you ever gotten caught up in the trap of religion or thought you had to keep a perfect rap sheet in order for God to be pleased with you?

I have. I've lived by that standard, and I didn't know I was doing it. But the truth is, living this way makes us almost entirely miss the beauty of the gospel and God's plan for us here on earth.

Here's what I mean: "All of us have become like one who is unclean, and all our righteous acts are like filthy rags; we all shrivel up like a leaf, and like the wind our sins sweep us away" (Isaiah 64:6).

Notice what Isaiah says in this verse: "our *righteous* acts are like filthy rags." He's not talking about the things we do that we know are wrong. In other words, apart from Jesus, even our good works are like filthy rags compared to God's standard. Pretty intense, huh?

Romans 3:10 adds: "No one is righteous—not even one" (NLT).

Bottom line: we *can't* be good enough. We can't earn God's approval by hitting the mark right every time. Our efforts still do not measure up to his standards. We still fall short. For all of us have fallen short of the glory of God (see Romans 3:23).

So where does that leave us? If even the "good" things we do aren't up to God's standards, how do we please him?

You're going to love the answer. (For some of you, it might even take a while to set in. And if you already know it, breathe in the reminder as I, too, need to do.)

Someone has already lived a perfect life for you, so you don't have to. You won't ever get to live the perfect life. But you get to live in the power and grace in which Jesus has covered you—if you have accepted him as your Savior.

Read that again and let it soak in.

That takes a lot of pressure off. God doesn't expect perfection out of you or me. I don't have to "be good enough" to earn his love. Jesus was good enough *for* me. The good works that we do are now pleasing to God because we do them covered in the righteousness of Jesus. Rather than seeing us in filthy rags, God now sees garments that are whiter than snow. And *that* glorifies the Father!

I've wrestled with this. I've thought of myself as good. I've expected that God must be pleased with me because I was the "good girl" who made good choices. Ha! I really didn't realize that those good works were still light-years away from the standard God has. Jesus was the only one who could meet those standards. Not Masey. Not you.

So what is our motivation for making good choices and doing good stuff? If Jesus already did everything for us, why do we have to?

As a child of God, you now get to glorify your Father. If you are truly his, it's impossible to constantly and habitually live as you did before you knew Christ. Yes, you will always mess up, but because the Holy Spirit lives inside of you now, he will always be refining you to look more and more like Jesus. That's why bad choices bother your spirit. That's why you can't escape the sinking feeling when you are living in sin. The Holy Spirit lives in you now. You're different. *You're a child of God.*

Jesus said, "You are the light of the world. A city set on a hill cannot be hidden. Nor do people light a lamp and put it under a basket, but on a stand, and it gives light to all in the house. In the same way, let your light shine before others, so that they may see your good works and give glory to your Father who is in heaven" (Matthew 5:14–16 ESV).

We are the light of the world. Light gives us the ability to see. Light lets us know what's around us, where we're walking, and what all is in the room.

We are the light for people to see Jesus.

We don't do good works because they earn us extra points with God. We do good works not to boast in self-righteousness or to make ourselves feel better, but we do them so that people can *see* the hope we have in us and *glorify* God!

If you've sinned against God in a blatant way, ask him to forgive you, turn from the sin, and live in the grace he covers you in. Don't live in the trap of shame. Jesus didn't live the perfect life and die for our sins so we could wallow in guilt. In the words of Taylor Swift, "shake it off" and keep walking!

Better yet, as Jesus says, your sins are forgiven: "Go and sin no more" (John 8:11 NLT).

If you have never accepted Jesus as your Savior and you feel a tugging at your heart—don't ignore it. That's the Holy Spirit drawing you in. Your life will never be the same and your eternity will be sealed in heaven. All you have to do is believe that God loved you so much that he sent his Son, Jesus, to come live the perfect life and die on a cross for your sins. On the third day he rose from the dead and defeated death. Because of that, you no longer have to fear anything in this world—not even death. His love has sealed you, and no matter what you've done, you are now covered in garments whiter than snow:

> For I am convinced that neither death nor life, neither angels nor demons, neither the present nor the future, nor any powers, neither height nor depth, nor anything else in all creation, will be able to separate us from the love of God that is in Christ Jesus our Lord. (Romans 8:38)

Day 3 Challenge

If you have accepted Jesus or want to talk more about it with someone, talk to a friend, parent, or anyone you know who is following Jesus. Tell them about your decision and send me a message via my website (maseymclainofficial.com) and let me know so I can celebrate with you!

If you are already a believer and feel as though you've been living in the trap of perfection or religion, I challenge you to surrender that to God. He doesn't want you to have it all together or to try to be perfect. He wants your heart—not perfection. Ask the Holy Spirit to guide you and shine through you in a way that glorifies God. I pray that you will live in that freedom.

*God, thank you that you don't hold me to a standard of perfection. Thank you that Jesus lived the perfect life for me and defeated death so I could be free and spend forever with you. Show me today how to glorify you and shine with the light you have put in me.*

# Three Important Things

You're an extraordinary person. You aren't meant for a mundane life. You aren't meant to just "get by" every day. You were made for a very specific purpose because you're a child of God. "For God has not given us a spirit of fear, but of power and of love and of a sound mind" (2 Timothy 1:7 NKJV).

I think one of the worst tricks of satan is to keep us from experiencing the power of God and to just stay comfortable and go through life. I can just hear him saying, *Sure you can believe, but don't do anything with it. Keep it in your quiet time and prayers. Life will be good. Go to church, make good choices, get a job, have a family, be a good person, enjoy life.* It's easy to think like this. And do you know why satan wants us to think this way?

Because we're not a threat to him when we're living comfortable lives.

I love 2 Timothy 1:7 because it reminds me of the power that lives in me that is capable of doing anything. Whatever I think I can't do, Christ in me can. When I'm scared, he's not. Through the power of the Holy Spirit living in me, he can truly do immeasurably more than anything I could ever imagine (see Ephesians 3:20). And that is true for every single child of God.

You have *not* been given a spirit of fear. Fear keeps you living a comfortable life. As a child of God you *have* been given a spirit of power, of love, and a sound mind.

What does that mean? That Christ wants to do extraordinary things through you. Going to church, having a quiet time, going to school, graduating, getting a job, and having a family are all wonderful things. They are all gifts from God. We should do those things!

But right in the middle of these everyday things, we must recognize the power that lives in us. We must realize what we are capable of through the power of the Holy Spirit. We have power to do *whatever* God calls us to do, no matter how impossible it seems. We have been given a spirit of love. That means that we can love those people that no one else will love. We can forgive those who seem impossible to forgive. We have been given a sound mind with which to make wise decisions and resist temptations.

Satan will attack all of these things because they make you a force for the kingdom of God and they threaten him.

Do you feel that you are just "getting by" or like you have been living too much of a comfortable life? Submit yourself wholly to God and tell him you want to live in the power, love, and mind-set he has called you to. Don't let the enemy keep you from living in the power of the Holy Spirit who lives in you.

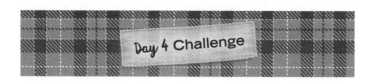

If you feel crippled by fear, remember the confidence and hope you have as a child of God. You are no longer a slave to fear. I challenge you to repeat the words of 2 Timothy 1:7 and to speak the name of Jesus over any area where you feel satan is crippling you with fear. Maybe you feel that you have just been cruising through life and living too comfortably. What if you decided to become a threat to the enemy, to allow your life to be a force in the kingdom of God? I also would encourage you to download the song "No Longer Slaves," sung by Jonathan David and Melissa Helser of Bethel Music. Sing it over your life. Pray against any spirit of apathy that is crippling you from living in your purpose.

Thank you, Lord, that you've called me, not to a mundane life, but rather to an extraordinary life through you. Don't let me be apathetic and just "get by." I want to live in the power, love, and mind-set you've given me.

Journal

# Make Room

Have the contents of your closet ever just completely exploded onto your floor and you had absolutely no idea how? I woke up to that one morning. The same thing can happen with the dishes in the sink. My sister and I have had many conversations about how I'm doing with keeping the sink clear and not letting the dishes sit (pathetic, I know, but I'm just being honest). Coming from someone with experience, let me tell you that if you ever happen to accidentally leave dishes in your sink when you go on a trip, fruit flies *will* find them. And if this ever happens, I highly recommend a how-to-destroy-fruit-flies tutorial on YouTube. After I went to war with the fruit flies in my kitchen, I decided it was time to do some deep cleaning. No more leaving dishes in the sink during weekend trips and no more piles of clothes all over my room. The cleaning up was no fun at all, but it felt so good afterward. My place was cozy and clean and had that *Ahhhhh!* feeling back.

I think our hearts sometimes get like my room and sink do. All you can think is, *What in the world happened? How did I get here? Why is my life so messy and chaotic and falling apart?* At times God seems far away, because there's so much clutter everywhere. Our hearts, which house the living God, get filled up with so many things that we think somehow belong. And we let them sit there.

So many things can distract us from living with purpose.

Make room. That's a word that the Lord has recently laid heavily on my heart. Make room for him to do his work. Make room for him to sit on his rightful throne in my heart. Sometimes it's just as simple as the Lord saying, "Go do the dishes, Masey. It's no coincidence there are so many fruit flies." He washes our hearts clean, but we are responsible for the never-ending pile of dishes.

I know I'm on a cleaning kick right now, but let's think for a minute about the process of cleaning the dishes. I usually rinse them off, load them into the dishwasher, put that magical little square soap thing in, shut it, turn it on, and let it do its work. It's the same with making room in my heart. When the Lord says it's time to "do the dishes," I have to start cleaning and getting rid of the junk and whatever is taking up space. What is filling up his home in my heart? I have to give it to him, trust him, and let him do his thing—just as the magical square detergent does its thing when all the dishes are finally put in the dishwasher. Not for one second do I doubt that the detergent will clean the dishes. So why do I doubt the power and goodness of God when I hand over the things he says have to go?

It can even be good things that are taking up space in my heart. But even good things don't have the right to sit on his throne.

Joshua 3:5 reads, "Consecrate yourselves, for tomorrow the LORD will do amazing things among you." Consecrate means "to make or declare holy." If they consecrate themselves, God wants to do *amazing things* with his people. They don't have to be perfect people, but they do have to be people who make room for him to work.

My home has the potential to be cozy, but I constantly leave clothes everywhere and dishes in the sink. God wants to blow my mind with what he wants to do, yet I don't always give him room. I want to declutter both my home and my heart. I want to make room for him. I want his temple to be holy. It can't happen by my own strength or righteousness, only by surrendering to the power of Christ in me.

He will clean the dishes only after I clear the sink.

Look at what Psalm 139:23–24 says: "Search me, God, and know my heart; test me and know my anxious thoughts. See if there is any offensive way in me, and lead me in the way everlasting." I challenge you to pray this prayer as David did. Ask God to search your heart and show you what needs to go. You might not want to hear it. But with the God of the universe living inside of you, there's too much on the line not to make room for him.

It might be cool to pray the words of this psalm every time you do the dishes or clean your room. He wants to do amazing things in and through you. Make room.

*God, thank you that you want to do amazing things in and through me. I don't want to have a cluttered heart that doesn't make room for you. "Search me, God, and know my heart; test me and know my anxious thoughts. See if there is any offensive way in me, and lead me in the way everlasting."*

Journal

# Entertainment

I love the entertainment industry and I really enjoy the idea of putting on a show for an audience. Whether it's a movie, music, a play . . . it's all just so much fun. I'm passionate about film acting, and I love writing music and performing.

A while ago I went on a date to a Johnny Cash show at the Legacy Theater in Peachtree City. There were times during the show when I was completely immersed in the music. My boyfriend and I were definitely the youngest couple at that Johnny Cash music show. But we loved it. The show started off a bit slow, but it got better as it went on. By the end I was wiping a tear because June was singing to Johnny about meeting him on the "Far Side Banks of Jordan" in heaven one day if she goes first. It was a much slower version than the original, and that made it a tearjerker for a sappy person like me. The performers did their job well. We left feeling that we'd seen a really great—even inspiring—show.

Entertainment provides an outlet to escape reality for just a little bit. You get to be immersed in someone else's reality on a TV screen or lost in your favorite song on the radio. It's fun, and it makes you dream. That's why I love it!

When you say you're "entertained" by something, you mean you thoroughly enjoy it. You allow yourself to sit for an hour or two, and even when the show starts a little slow, the more you watch, the more you are completely invested in it. You find yourself singing along or rooting for your favorite character or trying to figure out what's going to happen next. The entertainers have completely captured your attention.

Sometimes this works to our disadvantage. In my life, I have found that sin creeps in very quietly and without threat. Just as in the Johnny Cash show the other night, it starts slowly, but it gives me enough to keep my attention. Sin can start with a thought, a little compromise, something that doesn't draw much attention to itself. You say to yourself, *That's really not that big of a deal* or *Can you believe that person said that about me?* or *Does God* really *care if I do this?* Just one thought is enough for the enemy to get his foot in the door so you'll stay for the rest of the dramatic show. He knows we love entertainment, and he knows we like to get lost in a story. So naturally, we entertain thoughts, and those thoughts take us all kinds of places. Satan eggs us on: "Keep going; it gets way better." One thing leads to another, and we find ourselves so immersed in our own shows that we can't stop. All because of one seemingly innocent thought.

I'm convinced that satan is constantly trying to put on a show in our minds because our thoughts just don't stop. We make up scenarios in our minds in which our imaginations trump the truth. We bend the truth slightly and think, *It isn't hurting anyone.* We fail to guard our minds in purity, and slowly the boundaries disappear, because, *Well, I guess this isn't that bad.* We ruin friendships because, *I know what that person thinks about me.* We take those small thoughts and create all kinds of scenarios and let lies replace truth.

All the while, the show for satan is just beginning. While we entertain various thoughts, he feeds them and watches what happens. We start to self-destruct, and he's just grabbing popcorn. Do you get what I mean?

How can we fight back? Paul wrote this:

For though we live in the world, we do not wage war as the world does. The weapons we fight with are not the weapons of the world. On the contrary, they have divine power to demolish strongholds. We demolish arguments and every pretension that sets itself up against the knowledge of God, and we take captive every thought to make it obedient to Christ. (2 Corinthians 10:3–5)

That means any thought contrary to what Christ says must go—as soon as it enters our minds, before the show can even begin. I think it's easy to forget sometimes that we are actually in a war. We are fighting a battle with the enemy in our minds and hearts. But "the weapons we fight with are not the weapons of the world. On the contrary, they have divine power to demolish strongholds."

What are those weapons? The Bible says that Scripture is "sharper than any double-edged sword" (Hebrews 4:12). In other words, it's really great to fight with.

The psalms make great weapons. For instance, take Psalm 101:3: "I will set no worthless thing before my eyes; I hate the work of those who fall away; it shall not fasten its grip on me" (NASB). David was praying that he would not entertain worthless things, not set them before his eyes and enjoy them, and not let them fasten their grip on him. He knew they would only destroy him.

Instead of those thoughts, what should we entertain

in our minds? Paul gives us the answer: "Finally, brothers and sisters, whatever is true, whatever is noble, whatever is right, whatever is pure, whatever is lovely, whatever is admirable—if anything is excellent or praiseworthy— think about such things" (Philippians 4:8).

Entertainment is a wonderful thing, and I love it. However, in my short time here on earth, I have to make sure I am entertaining the right things. The smallest entertainment of a thought I know I shouldn't dwell on could lead to destruction. I need to trust the Holy Spirit inside of me, and trust his Word.

Lately I have been trying to work on this really hard. And let me just add that many times satan will attack even harder when you commit to working on something. When a thought that shouldn't be there comes to my mind, I quote Scripture. I ask God to help me. I tell him how weak I am and how much I need him. I tell him I don't want the enemy to win. I don't want to entertain him. "Keep your heart with all vigilance, for from it flow the springs of life" (Proverbs 4:23 ESV).

## Day 6 Challenge

Since we know that we're in a battle and satan is looking to distract us from living with purpose, let's not let him win. Remember one of the greatest weapons to fight with—Scripture. I challenge you to memorize 2 Corinthians 10:3–5. I'll do it too. More than that, I challenge you to memorize at least one verse from the Bible every week. You will be amazed at how God will use that in your life, and I truly believe you'll see just how powerful it can be to quote Scripture when you're struggling or tempted. Don't go through life not using the weapons God has given you. (Would you walk onto a battlefield without a weapon? I don't think so.)

*Lord, thank you that you give us what we need to fight the enemy. Don't let me go through life ignorant of how satan works and the ways he tries to distract me.*

Journal

# Ask for It

In my freshman year of high school, God began to teach me something simple but really profound. At some point that year someone challenged me to ask God to give me a desire to read his Word. At that time it wasn't something I craved or thought about much. I knew the stories in the Bible and my parents always taught me about Jesus, but I had never truly dived into it for myself. I was intrigued by the challenge: "Ask God to give you a desire for his Word."

OK. I began to do that. At the same time, I also disciplined myself to wake up a little bit earlier every day in order to read my Bible. The more I asked him to give me that desire, the more I found myself looking forward to spending time with him every morning. My appetite was growing every day, and I couldn't wait to fix myself a cup of coffee and cozy up in a blanket and spend that sweet time with him. I started to see my prayers being answered. I began to feel thrown off-balance and weird if I skipped a morning.

I could say with the psalmist: "How sweet are your words to my taste, sweeter than honey to my mouth! I gain understanding from your precepts; therefore I hate every wrong path. Your word is a lamp for my feet, a light on my path" (Psalm 119:103–105).

Those mornings with him shaped my heart throughout high school. I'm so thankful for the person who challenged me to pray for a desire to know God more and to spend time with him reading his Word. Those mornings were the preparation ground for what God had for me later down the road. I needed to have his Word planted in me. I needed to *know* him, not just know about him.

I've heard people say that they think the Bible is boring, they can't understand it, or they just don't have time. I beg you not to live by those excuses. They will keep you crippled. The enemy uses them to hold you back from realizing God's purpose in life. He wants to keep you living comfortably without the power the Word of God brings into your life: "The grass withers, the flower fades, but the word of our God stands forever" (Isaiah 40:8 NASB).

Remember, the most important thing you can do if

you want to live fully in your purpose is to seek the heart of God. This is a huge part of how you do that. Let God speak to you through the pages of his Word. Don't let your Bible just sit on your nightstand.

One of the best things about God is that we can ask him for things. And I mean more than, "help me do well on this test" or "help my neighbor's friend's cousin's cat that broke his leg." I'm talking game-changing things he can do in our hearts. It's just a beginning, but start by asking God to give you a bigger desire to know him and a bigger desire for his Word: "Ask and it will be given to you; seek and you will find; knock and the door will be opened to you. For everyone who asks receives; the one who seeks finds, and to the one who knocks, the door will be opened" (Matthew 7:7–8).

This verse doesn't mean God will give us whatever we want. Rather, he will give us what's in line with his plan, whatever we ask for that's within his will. And asking God to give you a desire to know him more through his Word is definitely in line with what he wills for your life.

Just as I was challenged to pray for a desire to read God's Word, I challenge you to pray the same thing. Don't be down on yourself if you don't have that desire right now. You can't create that desire on your own; only God can give it to you. But you can *ask* for it. If you take this challenge you also have another responsibility, and it requires discipline. It takes setting aside specific time to spend with him. Devotionals are beneficial, but never let them replace the richness of reading the Word of God. If you don't know where to start, try the book of John. Psalms is also a great starting place. You can read a little at a time; there's no pressure.

If you have trouble understanding the Bible, tons of resources are available, such as study Bibles with notes to help you understand the context of Scripture and to walk you through what each verse means. Some devotionals actually walk you through books of the Bible. (Check out books by Kelly Minter, Priscilla Shirer, and Beth Moore.) I would love to hear from you on my website about your journey with this and the way God works in your heart if you decide to take this challenge to ask God to create in you a desire for his Word.

*Lord, thank you that you speak to me through your Word.*
*I don't want to miss what you have to say and who you say*
*that you are in Scripture. Show me the power that it holds*
*in my life. Give me a hunger and a desire for your Word.*

```
     #250  04-04-2018 05:27PM
   Item(s) checked out to p31979713.

TITLE: The power [sound recording audiob
BRCD: 30646002755803
DUE DATE: 05-02-18

TITLE: It's worth it : 21-day devotional
BRCD: 30646003909649
DUE DATE: 05-02-18

TITLE: Living in the light : follow your
BRCD: 30646002929028
DUE DATE: 05-02-18

TITLE: The secret
BRCD: 30646003323858
DUE DATE: 05-02-18


        RIVERHEAD FREE LIBRARY
```

# What Determines Your Faith?

My greatest fear is being stranded out in the middle of the ocean. On a raft. With no drinking water. Surrounded by sharks. I just watched *Unbroken* recently, so if you're getting that mental image right now, that's what I'm picturing too. At the same time, I love to look at the ocean. It's unknown, it's massive, and it's beautiful. There's no telling what kind of creatures are swimming underneath the surface, but it's magnificent.

The scariest thing about the ocean is that there is no solid ground anywhere—unless you sink to the bottom, of course. So if I am ever stranded out at sea, I can think of only three options:

1. Swim as far as I can and most likely get so exhausted that I drown.

2. Wait on the raft to be rescued and most likely die of dehydration and sun poisoning.

3. Pray the Lord sends a whale to swallow me and spit me on the shore as he did with Jonah.

Basically, I'd be done for (unless I'm like the guy in *Unbroken* and I get rescued by a Japanese war boat and sent to a prison camp—which isn't much better).

In Mark 4, Jesus tells the disciples they are going to get in a boat to go to the other side. But at some point along the journey, a terrible storm comes up and almost kills them all. While the disciples are fighting for their lives as hard as they possibly can, they realize that *Jesus is asleep* in the boat.

The disciples wake Jesus up, and of course they ask, "Do you not care that we're drowning?"

The disciples had abandoned their normal lives to follow Jesus wherever he went. They had seen him do countless miracles. They believed he was powerful enough to do absolutely anything. Yet here he was asleep while they were fighting to stay afloat in the worst storm they'd ever experienced. They felt abandoned by Jesus.

I don't think they're the only ones who've ever felt that way.

Every time I've read this story, I've quickly glossed

over the "Jesus was asleep" part, focusing instead on the what he said to the disciples about not having any faith. I would always think, *You were on the boat with* Jesus. *How in the world could you doubt?* Ha.

Because of this bothersome part: *Jesus was asleep.* If I had been one of the disciples facing those massive waves, I would have said the same thing. I do it all the time: "Don't you care what's going on, Jesus? Don't you see me? Why are you letting me drown? Are you asleep? Do you even see what's going on right now?"

The storm was horrific. Water was filling up the boat, and there was nothing they could do about it. The disciples were about to drown. And yet Jesus' response when the disciples woke him up was a rebuke: "Why are you so afraid? Have you still no faith?"

Seems to me that the disciples had every reason to be afraid. Jesus was sleeping instead of helping them!

I've come to the conclusion that following Jesus does not always feel safe. In fact, our lives will not be easy. In *The Lion, the Witch, and the Wardrobe*, Lucy asks if Aslan is safe or not. This is Mr. Beaver's response: "'Safe?' said Mr. Beaver; '. . . Who said anything about safe? 'Course he isn't safe. But he's good.'"[*]

---

[*] C. S. Lewis, Goodreads, http://www.goodreads.com/quotes/81965-safe -said-mr-beaver-don-t-you-hear-what-mrs-beaver.

## It's Worth It

Following Jesus will not necessarily keep you safe. But he is always good.

Back to the boat and the horrified disciples. After Jesus woke up, he calmed the storm with one phrase: "Peace! Be still!" (Mark 4:39 ESV). And the winds and waves obeyed. Jesus had the power all along.

Even when it feels like I'm drowning and God has completely removed his presence from me, do I still trust him? Does he still hold the same power?

I love it when the presence of the Lord is strong, but I know those moments don't last forever. Sometimes when I feel he's near, I beg him to stay close, even though I know this feeling will go away. Ultimately, he will *never* leave me or forsake me (see Deuteronomy 31:6), although he'll withdraw himself in order for my faith to be strengthened.

He wants me to believe in him both when it feels like he's in the room, as well as when I can't feel him at all. He is *still on his throne*, regardless of how I feel. He sees the storm. He cares. He has never left me, and he never will.

I believe that Jesus purposefully fell asleep in the boat during the storm. After all, at the beginning of the story, Jesus is the one who told the disciples to go across to the other side. It wasn't even their idea.

Even though they knew they were exactly where Jesus wanted them to be, circumstances dictated the disciples' faith. The waves were too high, it was dark, and they were terrified. Circumstances told them not to believe and that Jesus didn't care about them. But the one they had been walking with was still the same. He still held the same power, whether he was awake or asleep. He would always be with them, as he will always be with us:

> Where shall I go from your Spirit? Or where shall I flee from your presence? If I ascend to heaven, you are there! If I make my bed in Sheol, you are there! If I take the wings of the morning and dwell in the uttermost parts of the sea, even there your hand shall lead me, and your right hand shall hold me. If I say, "Surely the darkness shall cover me, and the light about me be night," even the darkness is not dark to you; the night is bright as the day, for darkness is as light with you. (Psalm 139:7–12 ESV)

Jesus knew he wouldn't always be with the disciples physically and this was only the beginning of "storms" for them. They had to learn how to believe in his power, sovereignty, and presence no matter what was happening around them. I pray for that kind of faith too.

Day 8 Challenge

Maybe you feel as if God is a million miles away right now and doesn't care about the wind and the waves that are about to swallow you. Maybe you feel completely helpless and that he doesn't care. I challenge you to believe in his sovereignty and to trust in his love for you, no matter what your circumstances say. Nothing escapes his sight. He has not forsaken you. Call upon his name. Ask him to reveal his power, love, and comfort to you in the midst of your circumstances. Ask him to help you believe in his sovereignty, even if nothing seems to make sense right now.

*Lord, thank you that you promise in your Word never to leave me. Help me to remember that—even when it feels as though you have. Help me to trust your love for me and your sovereignty, even through storms. You alone hold the power to calm the wind and the waves, and everything is in your hands. No matter what, help me to remember that you are good.*

Journal

# Steady

The mountains—probably one of my favorite places to be! When you're up on a mountain, you kind of feel as if you're on top of the world; it's so peaceful, and the view is breathtaking. If I ever get to live my dream of living in a nice cozy house on top of a mountain, I think I'll probably turn into a crazy lady who never comes down.

First, though, you have to climb the mountain, and the worst part of the whole mountain experience is when you're about halfway up. Your legs start to feel like Jell-O, and the people hiking around you start looking at you funny because you're making loud, irregular breathing noises. (When you have your headphones on, you don't really realize how your breathing is disturbing the peace.)

It's the best feeling to get to the top. That's where I feel closest to the Lord, especially since I know Jesus loved mountains too. When Jesus needed to be alone to talk to the Father, the Bible says he went up a mountain.

However, I know that as wonderful as mountains are, life isn't lived on mountaintops.

Have you ever noticed how much more quickly you seem to go *down* a mountain than up? You almost have to run down because it's so steep. It can be pretty ruthless. And sometimes that's how life is. You keep climbing, climbing, climbing, pushing through, and pushing through until you get there. The summit is so, so sweet. Every step was worth it. But you know you have to come down at some point.

When you're on level ground, which is most of the time, the buildings and cars and trees and people don't look so small anymore, and taking on the world doesn't seem so easy. Reality sets in. The mundane, everyday tasks make you want to be back up on the mountain, where you felt close to God and everything looked perfect. Up there everything seemed so simple and beautiful, while down here all you see is what's around you.

I want to walk faithfully on level ground. That's something I am praying for every day.

If anyone in Scripture rode the highs and lows of life, it was David. One day he was the greatest and most loved king, and the next day everybody wanted him dead. Other days, he just cried out for the Lord to be near to him, because life was just confusing. He was no stranger to the mountain, and he was no stranger to level ground. He prayed: "Keep steady my steps according to your promise, and let no iniquity get dominion over me" (Psalm 119:133 ESV).

Yes, Lord. Keep *steady* my steps. Whatever the high, whatever the low, or however much level ground lies in front of me. According to your promise.

I am awful at directions. If it weren't for my GPS (which I endearingly named Florence, after *Florence and the Machine*—I thought it was clever), I'd be done for. There is a reason God put me in the twenty-first century.

I want God's Word to be my map for life, my GPS. It works when I'm walking on level ground, and it guides me up (and down) the mountain. Sometimes, when I'm on level ground, all I have is a memory of the view from up high. I can't see very far. I can start to panic and wonder what in the world is going on. But all he is asking me to do is to keep walking, to seek him and follow his Word. That's how he keeps our steps steady day after day: "He has told you, O man, what is good; and what does the Lord require of you but to do justice, to love kindness, and to walk humbly with your God?" (Micah 6:8 NASB). Walk humbly *with* your God. Through whatever lies ahead. In the mundane *now*.

## Day 9: Steady

I'll be the first to admit that I struggle with this some-times. I hate coming down from the "highs." Sometimes I get so frustrated. No matter how exciting, boring, or tedious the path may seem right now, all he's asking us to do is to walk with him. We just have to keep going and be faithful with whatever he's put in front of us. He honors that. Anyway—our decision to do that is really the only thing we have control over in this life.

Day 9 Challenge

Embrace the season of life you're in. _____
taintop or stuck on the plains ___ you can't ___
season of your life, memorize Micah 6:8 and try to practice it daily.
Do justice, love kindness, and walk humbly with your God.

*God, thank you that you want to walk beside me—in every
season, on every mountaintop, on level ground, and through
every valley. I want to walk next to you right now—on the
ground where I'm walking right now.*

Journal

# Make an Impact

I want to make an impact in the world, and I'm sure that you do too. In *I'm Not Ashamed,* remember what Rachel wrote when she was a little girl, when she traced her hand on the back of the drawer? She wrote, "These hands belong to Rachel Joy Scott and they will someday touch millions of people's hearts." Even as a little girl, Rachel seemed to know she was going to make an impact in the world; she just didn't know how.

One of my favorite things about Rachel was that she didn't wait for that "big moment" for God to use her to make a difference in the world. She didn't know that it would be through her death that millions of people would be affected by her life and what she left behind in her journals. She had no way of knowing that through her death, God would use her life to touch millions of people's hearts.

## Day 10: **Make an Impact**

What she *did* know was that she could make a difference right where God had placed her.

A few years ago when I was a freshman in college, I began to see that the Lord was teaching me what it truly looks like to make a difference in a way that matters. As I looked around me, I realized that my assignment, my chance to be used by God, was right in front of me. God had me where I was for a reason. So I began asking him to show me what to do where he had put me (rather than asking how to get where I wanted to be).

He began burdening my heart to lead a small group of high school girls at my church. They were the only group without a leader, and I knew without a doubt this was where the Lord wanted me. Getting to walk with these girls from their freshman year of high school to their senior year is still today one of the most rewarding things the Lord has ever allowed me to do. He taught me so many things through them, and I still love those girls with all of my heart. He taught me what it truly looks like to love people, not just to say you're going to pray for someone, but to really go to battle on their behalf. He showed me how to really care about the details of someone's life and how to walk with a person through whatever happens. I wouldn't trade that time for anything.

If you're like me and you're a dreamer, don't stop

dreaming. God made you that way for a reason. Dream big and go for it! But never forget to be faithful where God has put you now. Life has many different seasons, and you don't want to miss God's blessings or what he wants to teach you. You have an assignment *right now*, a chance to experience God in ways you could never have imagined.

Rachel Scott was a student at Columbine High School. She had a big dream in her heart for the Lord to use her in a mighty way. Yet she was faithful at Columbine High School to love those around her and to shine brightly where God had placed her. She didn't view her time there as one of waiting for a big opportunity or a special platform. She didn't just pass by other students in the halls; she was present, and she truly saw them. She saw their hurt, their struggles, and their hearts. And she reached out to them, loving them. She truly became the hands and feet of Jesus to people *right where God had her*—in her school.

That's how she made an impact and that's how we can too.

Someday, we will stand before God:

"Then the King will say to those on his right, 'Come, you who are blessed by my Father; take your inheritance, the kingdom prepared for you since the creation of the world. For I was hungry and you gave me something to eat, I was thirsty and you gave me something to drink, I was a stranger and you invited me in, I needed clothes and you clothed me, I was sick and you looked after me, I was in prison and you came to visit me.'

"Then the righteous will answer him, 'Lord, when did we see you hungry and feed you, or thirsty and give you something to drink? When did we see you a stranger and invite you in, or needing clothes and clothe you? When did we see you sick or in prison and go to visit you?'

"The King will reply, 'Truly I tell you, whatever you did for one of the least of these brothers and sisters of mine, you did for me.'" (Matthew 25:34–40)

Day 10 Challenge

What if you decided to not just pass through life but to commit to making a difference in the people God has put around you? What if you decided to make an impact right where you are? Ask God to help you see others the way he sees them. Look for the ones who don't have any friends. Keep your eyes open to those who are hurting. Sit with them and get to know them. Let God use *you* to show his love to them.

*God, thank you that you that you want to use me to make a difference. Give me eyes to see people the way you see them. Break my heart for what breaks your heart, and put into my heart a love for the people you have placed around me.*

Journal

# One Thing That Will Never Be Taken Away

Luke tells a great short story about two women named Mary and Martha. Imagine two sisters who just heard the news that Jesus is actually coming to their home. Pretty exciting day, right? Take your time reading the short passage:

> As Jesus and his disciples were on their way, he came to a village where a woman named Martha opened her home to him. She had a sister called Mary, who sat at the Lord's feet listening to what he said. But Martha was distracted by all the preparations that had to be made. She came to him and asked, "Lord, don't you care that my sister has left me to do all the work by myself? Tell her to help me!"
>
> "Martha, Martha," the Lord answered, "you are worried and upset about many things, but few

things are needed—or indeed, only one. Mary has chosen what is better, and it will not be taken away from her." (Luke 10:38–42)

I can't help but laugh and also feel sympathetic towards Martha. I can just imagine a frustrated and frazzled Martha running around the house, so annoyed at her sister's lack of concern about the work. Especially since this is no ordinary guest in their house—it's *Jesus*.

Although it's wonderful that Martha opened her home to Jesus, the Savior of the world, she was concerned with everything else *except* spending time with him. Overwhelmed by what needed to be done, she missed everything that was important about his being there.

How many times do we do the same thing? We check everything off our to-do list and miss out on sitting at the feet of Jesus. Our lives are filled with many distractions, and there is a never-ending cycle of things to do every single day.

But there was Mary, sitting at the Lord's feet and listening to what he said. Didn't she realize there was a lot to do? Yep. But *Jesus* had come, and she didn't want to miss a minute of the time he would spend with them, no matter what needed to be done.

Jesus' response to Martha when she complained about

Mary is his response to all of us today: "You are worried and upset about many things, but few things are needed—or indeed, only one. Mary has chosen what is better, and it will not be taken away from her."

Like us, Martha was worried and upset about so many things that didn't really matter. Soaking in the presence of her Savior would have given Martha everything she needed, and it would have been so much better than checking off a to-do list or trying to impress people.

"What Mary has chosen will not be taken away from her." That's my favorite line. Life will be endlessly busy. But everything on this earth is temporary. The presence of God, however, is permanent. And believers can rest assured that his presence will never be taken away from them, no matter what happens in life. Just as he told Mary.

When I say or think, "I didn't have my quiet time today" or "I haven't had time to talk to God at all today," I'm the one who loses. But when I *make* time to do those things, no matter how busy my schedule is, I actually tend to get more done that day and things don't seem so chaotic! Funny how that works.

If you feel like Martha and are overwhelmed, anxious, tired, or just need a break, I would encourage you to just stop and sit at the feet of Jesus. Soak in his presence and listen to his words. Turn on some worship music and just sit in his presence. Let him fill you up with what you need. Don't miss him sitting in your house.

As the band For King and Country puts it, "There is never a convenient time to do something important."* You can't wait for a break in your work before you sit in his presence. Regardless of all the things you have to do every single day, make time to sit at his feet—it's worth it. Life gets hectic, but spending time in his presence will always fill you up and soothe your mind and heart. *And that will not be taken away from you.*

---

* For King and Country, *Twitter*, October 7, 2015, https://twitter.com /4kingandcountry/status/651814218270806016.

Day 11 Challenge

I know you have a never-ending list of things you have to get done. That's reality, and those things are important. But I challenge you to just stop for a few moments today. Turn on a worship song or go on a walk and just pray. Turn off your mind and put your list and phone away for just a bit, and let him fill you up.

*Thank you, Jesus, for your presence. Thank you that it fills me up with what I need. Help me not to miss out on you being in my house because of everything else I feel has to be done first.*

Journal

## Day 12

# A Day
# I'll Never Forget

"What was your favorite scene to film in *I'm Not Ashamed?*" That's another question I get asked quite a bit. The answer sometimes comes as a shock to people, and honestly, it came as a shock to me.

It's the scene where the shooters put a gun to Rachel's head and ask if she "still believes in [her] God." Playing that scene was both the most special and the most heart-wrenching experience I've ever had. I'll never forget it.

To be honest, I was really nervous about that day. That scene is why Rachel is considered a martyr for Christ. We all knew what we were about to film, but we had no idea what God was about to do.

The weight of what we were about to portray was evident to everyone from the moment we stepped onto the set that day. But that morning I knew the Lord's hand was on

74

## Day 12: *A Day I'll Never Forget*

us. I remember waking up with a sense of peace. The Lord brought me to the story of Stephen, the first martyr mentioned in Scripture. I knew then that his presence would be with us, and he would give us everything we needed.

Take a look at Stephen's last moments:

When the members of the Sanhedrin heard this, they were furious and gnashed their teeth at him. But Stephen, full of the Holy Spirit, looked up to heaven and saw the glory of God, and Jesus standing at the right hand of God. "Look," he said, "I see heaven open and the Son of Man standing at the right hand of God."

At this they covered their ears and, yelling at the top of their voices, they all rushed at him, dragged him out of the city and began to stone him. Meanwhile, the witnesses laid their coats at the feet of a young man named Saul.

While they were stoning him, Stephen prayed, "Lord Jesus, receive my spirit." Then he fell on his knees and cried out, "Lord, do not hold this sin against them." When he had said this, he fell asleep. (Acts 7:54–60)

I have never felt the Lord's presence as strongly as I did in those moments of filming. It felt as if God was allowing me to see into a window of what Rachel experienced that day. I knew how much his heart broke, but at the same time how proud he was of her; I could feel his arms wrapped around me the entire time. It seemed as though God did that to show me a glimpse of what she must have felt that day, in the pain and suffering, with the Lord's love surrounding her. I truly believe that Jesus stood for Rachel in the same way he did for Stephen when the heavens opened up.

Even now, it's hard to put into words how it felt to film that scene. It's still the most special day I've ever experienced.

Like a lot of people, I wonder what I would do in the last few moments of my life. If a gun were pointed to my head, would I still say I believe in God?

I believe Rachel was able to say yes because she'd gotten to a place in her life where she knew he was worth it. The world left her empty, but Jesus satisfied her soul. He was everything to her.

Rachel said, "Jesus gave his life for me, and I will give my life to him."

Is he everything to you?

Day 12 Challenge

I challenge you to ask Jesus to become everything to you. Pray for the kind of faith that Stephen, Rachel, and countless other people around the world today have. It's a weighty prayer; understandably, it may take some time to pray it. Praying this way doesn't mean you're going to have to give your life tomorrow—or that you'll ever be in a situation like Rachel's. Most of us won't ever be. But it means you want a heart that will follow your Shepherd, no matter what happens in life. He's worth it to you.

Maybe you can't pray that yet, honestly. Maybe it scares you to pray something like that, or maybe you just don't fully understand it all. It's OK to tell God that too. Ask the hard questions. Wrestle with it. Talk to him about your heart, whatever state it may be in. He wants to know it all.

*Jesus, you leave me in awe. Thank you that no matter what happens in this life, you hold my eternity in your hands, and nothing can separate me from your love. Thank you for giving your life for me. I want you to become everything to me.*

Journal

# The Key

Recently I bought a key. Not the sort of key you use to get in a house, but a key on a chain that I wear as a necklace. It has the word *Strength* on it and it serves as a reminder of something I don't want to forget.

Ask anyone in my family, and they will tell you that I am not physically strong. I consider myself athletic, but I have absolutely no upper-body strength. To put it in perspective, my little brother has always been able to beat me up.

Strength is something I know I don't have. No one has to tell me I'm not strong. If I try to pick up something too heavy, I know I'll drop it. Lots of people can relate—except those chicks in the action movies. (It's a dream of mine to be in an action movie and kick down a door or something.)

I think often about how strong God is. He knows I'm

not strong. He knows every single weakness I have. And God, being the most amazing gentleman ever, says he will carry heavy things for me. Not only does he carry them, he doesn't drop a thing. No matter what the impossible situation, task, or struggle, he can carry it. He just asks me to trust him.

That's why I love 2 Corinthians 12:9 (ESV): "But He said to me, 'My grace is sufficient for you, for my power is made perfect in weakness.' Therefore I will boast all the more gladly of my weaknesses, so that the power of Christ may rest upon me."

What does it mean to boast about our weaknesses? Paul didn't mind telling others he was weak. He knew that any good that anyone could see in him came from Christ. He knew he was not righteous apart from Jesus and that he needed to rely on him every single day. Paul knew that whatever God called him to do, he *had* to do through the power of Holy Spirit working in and through him. He could boast about his human weaknesses, because they made it possible for God to show his strength.

Because Paul believed this, God used him in incredible ways.

When I began filming *I'm Not Ashamed*, I knew that if my source of strength didn't come from God, I would fail. I knew I wasn't strong enough or confident enough to play such an emotionally driven roller coaster role. It was intimidating to portray a real person—especially one whose mom would be on set often.

But Jesus is always confident. And he is always strong. And he carried me through. Every day I had to put my confidence in the Lord and not rely on my own abilities. I have been an actress for a while and have been trained in my craft, but I could not, on my own, portray what needed to be shown in this film. Every single day I had to surrender to him and trust that he would carry me and give me everything I needed.

The words of this psalm became my own: "The LORD is my strength and my shield; my heart trusts in Him, and I am helped; therefore my heart exults, and with my song I shall thank Him. The LORD is their strength, and He is a saving defense to His anointed" (Psalm 28:7–8 NASB).

Our strength is the Lord. We never have to be strong enough. We never have to carry the weight of our circumstances. Jesus carries them for us. He simply asks us to trust in him and let him carry what we cannot:

He gives strength to the weary and increases the power of the weak. Even youths grow tired and weary, and young men stumble and fall; but those who hope in the Lord will renew their strength. They will soar on wings like eagles; they will run and not grow weary, they will walk and not be faint. (Isaiah 40:29–31)

Admit that you are weak. Believe that he is strong. And let him carry you.

That is the key.

Usually when God calls us to do something, it's not easy. He doesn't call us to easy assignments that we can do on our own without him. Have you ever heard, "God won't give you more than you can handle?" I would argue with that and say *yes, he will.* When he gives you more than you can handle, you have to rely on him to help you. And there isn't *anything* that *he* can't handle! When impossible tasks come your way, let him do his job to carry you through them. Trust him. Admit to him your weakness and acknowledge his strength. Let him amaze you.

∞

*Lord, thank you that you are strong. Thank you that you don't leave me to do the impossible, but you carry me through it. You never call me to do something and leave me up to my own abilities. I trust you, and I ask that your power work through me to do what I can't on my own.*

Journal

This is the best hair and makeup team ever—Cat and Velvet

School

The Squad

The one and only, #Celine

Name that scene

Team. Behind every scene, Director Brian Baugh was right there walking with me through every emotion in every scene.

The beautiful and talented Jennifer O'Neil gave me
a lot of valuable advice from her career as an actress.

Coffee shop scene

Big Bro'

I never thought I'd get to go to prom again. Everyone had a blast!

The wardrobe team made an exact replica of
Rachel's prom dress and did my hair to look like hers.

The Class of 1999. This was one of the most fun days of filming.

Daniel (who played Austin) was always makin' me smile.

Daniel and I. He knew my lines better in this scene than I did.

Fun fact: every week on our one day off, we played basketball.

The day we filmed Rachel's last moments before she died; I will never forget that day.

We all walked away impacted by Rachel's story.

Before Emma did her scene at the car. Love her.

Stepping into Rachel's shoes was the most humbling and rewarding experience I've ever had.

# Hollow

Definition of *hollow*: having a hole or empty space inside; lacking significance.

One of my favorite songs right now is "Hollow" by Tori Kelly. If you don't already know it, you should go straight to iTunes and download it. The simple lyrics are a profound, beautiful reminder of the only one who can fill the space in us that craves to be satisfied.

Without Jesus, we're hollow.

I have a beautiful friend who has a way of making sense of things. She likes to use simple analogies that always leave me thinking. Jesus has captivated her heart, and everyone around her can see it. He's brought her out of some really difficult things, and she's one of those people who thinks before she speaks and articulates the faithfulness of God in her life so well to others. One day she said, "All of us have these God-shaped holes inside. We constantly try to fill them with stuff, but the only thing that can fill up a God-shaped hole is God."

So simple, but so true. How many times throughout a day are we constantly trying to fill that God-shaped hole, that hollowness inside of us? We try to fill it with love, acceptance, romantic interests, social media, popularity, jobs, friends, success—the list could go on and on. And you know what, every time I try to fill the hollow space in my heart up with these things, I'm left feeling empty, purposeless, and alone. They just don't work.

I'm left hollow.

John 4:1–30 describes a woman who had a pretty terrible reputation. For starters, she was known for "getting around." But Jesus offers something to the woman that day that completely changes everything for her: "Jesus said to her, 'Everyone who drinks of this water will be thirsty again, but whoever drinks of the water that I will give him will never be thirsty again. The water that I will give him will become in him a spring of water welling up to eternal life'" (John 4:13–14 ESV).

The woman at the well was just an empty, searching soul, trying to fill up the hollow space in her heart. But none of her efforts worked. Every man she had ever tried to

## Day 14: Hollow

find fulfillment and purpose in gave her the same result—
temporary satisfaction that only left her empty. What Jesus
offered her that day, would change everything for her.
Only his love could fill her empty cup.

I struggle with this a lot sometimes. I try to fill up the hollow space in my heart with the temporary distractions that continually seem to vie for my attention. I know I wasn't created for these things—and I know we weren't created to feel empty either. Are you drinking from the well of living water that Jesus offers, or are you trying to quench your thirst with water that will leave you thirsty again? It's an everyday choice. Let him satisfy the hollow space in your soul that only he can fill.

*God, thank you that you never leave me feeling empty. Thank you that you created me to live filled up by your presence and truly satisfied by you alone. Forgive me for trying to fill my God-shaped hole with other things. Only your love can fill up my cup.*

Journal

# Talents

When I was growing up, I tried a ton of different activities to figure out what I was good at. My mom was a fantastic dancer when she was younger, the kind of dancer who would win national competitions. She just had a natural ability, and she worked to develop it. So as a little girl I decided I wanted to try out dancing too. I got a tutu and ballet shoes. Mom was good, so I would definitely be good, too, right?

No. I was a pretty scrawny kid, and my long arms and legs refused to be graceful. My poor mom would smile and encourage me, but I quickly found out I was not cut out to be a ballerina. It was too slow for me, anyway. I would rather put on a princess dress, hop on my mini dirt bike, and go save the world in my backyard. I had no time for tutus and graceful movements.

## Day 15: Talents

Then there was the time I tried to be a gymnast. Once again, lanky arms and legs do not work in this sport. You need to be strong and compact and have the ability to flip over quickly. Not me. I got tired of landing on my head every time I tried a back handspring, and I gave up.

Later on, I finally found my niche when I joined sports teams and also acted in plays in school.

Finally.

Did you know the Bible also talks about talents? In Matthew 25:14–25, Jesus is talking about what the kingdom of God is like. It is too long to quote here, so you will have to read it on your own in order to understand the rest of today's devo.

During biblical times, a *talent* was the largest unit of currency. It was a measurement for weight equal to about seventy-five pounds. When someone was given a talent, it was a big deal.

At the beginning of the story, look how much the master trusted his servants. He gave talents to each servant according to their ability to handle the assets. He trusted his servants to steward the wealth wisely and faithfully.

Here's what they did: "He who had received the five talents went at once and traded with them, and he made five talents more. So also he who had the two talents made two talents more" (vv. 16–17 ESV). These two servants took what they had and multiplied it—*immediately*. (Note that they traded and doubled their talents "at once.")

After he returned, when the master saw what the man with five talents had done, he replied, "Well done, good and faithful servant. You have been faithful over a little; I will set you over much" (v. 21).

And the servant who had received the two talents was faithful to do the same as the servant who had five. He did not complain to the master that he was not given as much, but instead he took what he had and did the best he could with it. The master's response was the same to him: "Well done, . . . I will set you over much" (v. 23).

But the servant who was only given one talent "went and dug in the ground and hid his master's money" (v. 18). Later, when the servant told his master what he had done, the master was not pleased. Whether his actions were motivated by fear and distrust or apathy and laziness, the master was not happy with the servant's choice to do nothing. His actions were not wise; they communicated that he had no desire to please his master.

And he received no reward.

What about the talents that you and I have been given by our master? How are we stewarding our God-given abilities, dreams, desires, and responsibilities?

## Day 15: Talents

Are we more worried about what we have not been given instead of investing in what we've been given?

We all have been created for a reason and have been given a great responsibility as children of God. We are all gifted in different ways to glorify God and we have been given different areas of influence and people to love and point to Jesus. And each of us has been allotted a certain amount of time to steward what we have been given.

What talents have you been given to use to glorify God? Who are the people around you that you can love and point to Jesus? What is your area of influence?

Please, if you think you do not have much influence or that what you do does not matter, you are believing a lie from the enemy. The unfaithful servant thought that, and he was so wrong. You *have* been given talents to steward, no matter how big or small. God will notice what you do with them. He expects you to be faithful.

Whatever gifts you have been given, work at them with all your heart, as working for the Lord and not for people (see Colossians 3:23).

Remember, don't wait for God to use you in a big way; instead, make an impact now. Being faithful with your talents is one of the ways to do that. Do you want to do something great with your life one day? Do you want to make a difference being a teacher, a dancer, an actress, an entrepreneur, or a pastor? Keep in mind what the master said: "You have been faithful with little; I will set you over much." I challenge you to be faithful with the talents you have right now, however big or small they are. It matters what you do with them.

*Jesus, thank you that you told this parable to remind me about the importance of what you've given me to steward. I want to be faithful with my talents. Help me to be able to recognize what those talents are, and show me how to steward them well.*

Journal

## Day 16

# Teasing

No, I'm not talking about your hair. When I think of teasing, I think of someone dangling something in front of me but never letting me quite take hold of it. Or I think of the girl or guy who flirts just enough to get someone's attention, then leaves the person hurt and confused.

And sometimes, I think of God.

Sometimes I think God has a string with all of my dreams, hopes, and desires on it. He just dangles them down from heaven, then snatches his hand back up before I have time to enjoy or experience them. Have you ever felt like that?

There was a time in my life when this happened a lot. I was constantly frustrated. It seemed as though every time I got close to something, all of a sudden the door would close. Dream jobs, relationships, new opportunities—lots of doors slammed shut.

## Day 16: Teasing

The worst part was how many times I truly felt that God was the one who was opening all those doors in the first place. I couldn't help but think, *Why lead me this far, only to say no?*

To be honest, I was mad and frustrated. I couldn't get rid of this mental image of God teasing me. So *many* closed doors? Why would he bring me almost close enough to touch a dream, and then *bam. Sorry, wrong door, Mase.* I can't sugar-coat it. That attitude (which I'm not all that proud of) seems disrespectful to God, doesn't it?

Because I was carrying this view of him, I went in to things fearfully. Whenever I would start to feel his blessing in something, I would brace myself for a crash: "Here it goes. . . . Is this gonna end, too, Lord?" Operating under a mind-set like this, I was bound to feel lost in almost every category of my life.

One day I read Jesus' words: "Seek first the kingdom of God and His righteousness, and all these things shall be added to you" (Matthew 6:33 NKJV).

Seek *first* the kingdom of God. Was I seeking God? Honestly, yes. I was seeking him a lot. But was I seeking open doors and a yes from him more?

The answer is way too easy.

What does it mean to seek the kingdom of God then? I prayed for God's will *all* the time. I spent time with him every day and I tried to honor him with the way I lived. I couldn't figure out when I got off the track. How had my view of him gotten so distorted, to the point that I couldn't get rid of it?

I think my biggest problem was that I was too concerned with what the Lord had for me. I was so obsessed with "finding out God's will" and figuring out what I was supposed to do, that I forgot about my true purpose—which is to seek his kingdom. To glorify him. To serve and love others.

One day I was at a voice lesson, and my voice teacher stopped me mid-song and just looked at me. She said, "Masey, you are so concerned with 'getting it right' that I'm scared you're losing your natural, true voice. Let go, and just sing."

Suddenly God was speaking to me with a megaphone, loud and clear: *You are so concerned with figuring out what's next or where I'm leading. Just walk with me.*

I had to let go and start truly trusting him with my dreams, my relationships, and my plans. I had to lay them all down. And I had to change my view of God back to what is true. One day my mom found me crying in my room, and with such love and wisdom she said, "Masey, don't look any further than the cross." It helped. Finally, once I started trying to do that every single day, the word *tease* began to be replaced with the word *love*.

## Day 16: Teasing

Why would a God who loved me enough to die for me on the cross want to tease, confuse, and hurt me? He wouldn't. The cross has a way of putting everything in perspective, right?

He is so good.

I found something else that Jesus had said: "If you, then, though you are evil, know how to give good gifts to your children, how much more will your father in heaven give good gifts to those who ask him!" (Matthew 7:11).

He *delights* in giving us good things. We don't have to be timid to ask for and accept those gifts out of fear that he'll snatch them away or keep them dangling in front of us to tease us. He *loves* giving us good things, and he is always working for our good. Just as a parent does for a child (but times a million). This is true, no matter which doors he opens or closes.

Ever since I refocused my mind and started truly *trusting* him, I have felt free. I still struggle sometimes and he is constantly teaching me surrender, but that's when I have to meditate on what I know is true. It's kind of crazy how I can now look back on every single door he closed and see exactly why he closed it. He wasn't teasing me after all; he was protecting me. He wasn't taking my dreams away from me; he was waiting to blow my mind with what he had for me: "And we know that in all things God works for the good of those who love him, who have been called according to his purpose" (Romans 8:28).

Don't take that Scripture lightly. Believe it. Stand on it. If doors are closing right now and your dreams are crumbling right in front of you, hold on. Don't let your view of God get distorted. He is *always* good. He sees. There are doors that will open that you never could have even imagined, and there are doors he might close for a season, but open back up when the time is right. Seek *him* without seeking answers for a little while, and see what he will do. Seek his kingdom *first;* he will take care of the rest:

> Give thanks to the LORD, for he is good! His faithful love endures forever. (Psalm 107:1 NLT)

> Every good and perfect gift is from above, coming down from the Father of the heavenly lights, who does not change like shifting shadows. (James 1:17)

Don't let your view of God get distorted. We have never been promised that life won't be hard, but we have been promised that he is good. Remind yourself of who God says he is, and dwell on that. His loving character *never* changes. If you've been seeking answers from God more than you have been seeking God himself, I challenge you to stop for a little while. Instead, seek *him*, apart from the answers.

*Lord, thank you that your Word reminds me of who you are. Help me to cling to your unchanging character, no matter what life looks like around me. You are good. Your love for me never changes and never ends. Help me to seek you and your kingdom above seeking any answers in my life.*

Journal

# focus

Let your eyes look directly forward,
and your gaze be straight before you.
*Proverbs 4:25 ESV*

*f*ilming *I'm Not Ashamed* was the most powerful experience of my life, and I'm constantly in awe of all the Lord
did while we were filming. One of the greatest things I
learned while filming is how important it is to stay focused.
When you are the lead in a film and have to work twelve
to sixteen hours every single day and are in almost every
scene, you can't really have an off day. Whatever you bring
to the table that day will be on a film forever. You have to
stay focused. Every scene counts.

In film acting, it takes a *lot* of time just to film one scene.
There are so many different angles, shots, and viewpoints.
You have to do a scene over and over again until every angle

is shot and all the actors and actresses have given their best performance. Everybody has to stay focused.

Before I went to Nashville to film, a very talented actress gave me some very helpful advice. She said, "When you are on set, don't get distracted. Yes, you will want to talk to everyone and have fun and socialize between takes, but you have a very big responsibility. Figure out where your character needs to be emotionally, work to get there, and just stay there until the scene is completely done." She continued to explain that if I didn't do that, I would make the work ten times harder on myself, because I would have to get back in the zone every time the scene started up again: "It's so much easier to stay in it and see how far you can go."

That's the best professional advice I have ever gotten. I need to recall those words every single day. I can't help but relate this to our walk with Jesus: "You keep him in perfect peace whose mind is stayed on you, because he trusts in you" (Isaiah 26:3 ESV).

How much difference could it make in our lives if we would only stay focused? I can tell you that if I had not received this advice for acting, I would not have been able to give the delivery I wanted to. I would have never known how much freedom there can be with laser-like focus. Once I was "in the zone," I could explore all of the levels

I could take my character to in a scene. I could go deeper and deeper in every take, without having to get back into character each time, because I was already there.

I notice how this works in my walk with Christ. When I am truly walking with him every day, focused on my purpose and leaning in to what he is doing and saying, it's so much easier to hear from him and to walk in what he has for me.

It is far too easy to call "Cut!" in our walk with him and to get lazy.

God wants to take us deeper and deeper, to give us the freedom to walk in all that he has for us. But we can't jump in and out of it as we please.

Just as I cannot lose my focus between takes and expect a great performance, I have to "stay in the zone" with God.

One of the greatest things in film acting happens when you and the other actors are so immersed in the characters that if your scene partner does something different from what is in the script, you know exactly how to respond because you're 100 percent present in that moment. No matter what unexpected twist happens in the scene, you can react honestly, because both of you are in the zone.

In our walk with Jesus, I wonder if we would be less thrown off by twists and turns if we just stayed in the zone. If we were so immersed in truth, no matter what satan tries to trip us up with or what lies he throws our way, we would know exactly how to respond because we are walking so close with Jesus.

I have no idea what anything looks like on camera after a day of filming, but I do know if I gave it my all and if I was 100 percent present in the scenes. As believers, we should approach our lives the same way. When it is all said and done, we cannot go back and redo the scenes of our lives and the stories that we lived out any more than an actress can redo scenes once a film is out.

I pray that each of you will live with a focus that frees you and beautifies your walk with God. I want you to be so immersed in living for his glory that the world will see a beautiful and breathtaking performance that points straight to Jesus: "Let your eyes look directly forward, and your gaze be straight before you" (Proverbs 4:25 ESV).

Day 17 Challenge

Stay in it. Today, don't hop in and out of the scenes you find yourself in. Can you make a habit of staying focused, so the enemy's tactics don't throw you off and you don't fall for his distractions? Do you want to go deeper and deeper and find yourself on a whole new level of focus and intimacy with God? It's possible, with his help, and I challenge you today to start making a habit of it. Write yourself a note and post it on your mirror. Maybe it should simply say, "Stay focused." Don't forget that the enemy is at work, trying to see how he can derail you next. Today and every day, be conscientious and *stay focused.*

᠅

*Lord, thank you that I have the opportunity to go deeper and deeper with you. I don't have to settle for a life that's mediocre, but I can truly experience You. I don't want to settle for anything less. Help me to stay focused.*

Journal

## Day 18

# If You follow Your Heart

When I was little, I loved a movie called *Thumbelina*. Actually, I still love it (along with most every other Disney animated movie). In it, a fairy meets a fairy prince who saves her from all kinds of scary creatures in the woods, and they end up living happily ever after. Does it get any better than that? Like I said, I really love Disney.

In the movie, there's a song called "Follow Your Heart." I used to fly around my house like a fairy and sing it at the top of my lungs, loud and proud. But one day my mom gently said, "Masey, I know you love that song, but always remember, it's not your heart you follow, it's Jesus. Your heart won't lead you where you want to go."

Cue an eye roll and, "Mom. It's just a song . . ."

Even though I didn't really understand what she was saying that day, I always, always remembered it.

"Follow your heart." We hear that from the time we are little. If your heart wants it, it must be right. If it makes you feel good, then follow it. Right?

That isn't what God says. "The heart is deceitful above all things, and desperately sick; who can understand it?" (Jeremiah 17:9 ESV).

Bottom line: Our hearts can't be trusted. When sin entered the world, human hearts became tainted with desires that aren't from God. Jesus is the one who purifies our hearts and makes them clean. He's the only one who is trustworthy to follow. Apart from him, you really cannot trust your heart.

Have you ever been in a situation where what you were doing felt really good and your heart definitely wanted it? Maybe you were in a relationship with someone who made your heart skip a beat, but you knew you shouldn't pursue it. Maybe you were listening to music that made you feel good, but at the same time it bothered you inside. Maybe you were messing around with someone, but you knew it wasn't right. Sometimes our hearts and emotions can lead us down a wrong path.

I've noticed how often my heart will urge me toward things that are contrary to God's will. And any time I have followed what my heart wants and it doesn't line up with what God wants, I end up in a mess.

## Day 18: If You Follow Your Heart

At the same time, God can use the desires of your heart in beautiful ways when your heart has been submitted to him. How can you know if your heart is in a good place or not? How do you know what to follow?

Jesus said, "Where your treasure is, there your heart will be also" (Luke 12:34).

That means if God is your ultimate treasure and your heart is fully surrendered to him, your heart will begin to line up with his desires.

The psalmist wrote: "Delight yourself in the LORD, and he will give you the desires of your heart" (Psalm 37:4 ESV). This doesn't mean that the Lord will give you all that your heart is desiring *right now*. It means that if you delight yourself in the things of God, the desires in your heart will change to look like his desires.

Apart from God, our hearts are "desperately sick" (Jeremiah 17:9 ESV). Desperately sick hearts call evil good, and good evil. That's why the world lives opposite from how God says to live. Without God, we follow choices made with "desperately sick" hearts.

The Old Testament prophet Isaiah addressed this: "Woe to those who call evil good and good evil, who put darkness for light and light for darkness, who put bitter for sweet and sweet for bitter" (Isaiah 5:20).

So what can we do? We must line ourselves up with

truth. Feelings and emotions are great; you just can't make all of your decisions based on them. That's why God gave us his Word—to guide our hearts: "Create in me a pure heart, O God, and renew a steadfast spirit within me" (Psalm 51:10).

I have turned one of my favorite lines in an old hymn into a prayer: "Bind my wandering heart to Thee."* I pray that all the time because I know what my heart is capable of without him.

---

\* Robert Robinson, "Come, Thou Fount of Every Blessing," *A Collection of Hymns Used by the Church of Christ in Angel Alley* (Bishopgate, UK: 1759), http://hymntime.com/tch/htm/c/o/m/e/comethou.htm.

Surrender your heart to God. Your emotions, your feelings, your desires, your temptations, your struggles—all of it. Delight yourself in him, and watch how he will change your heart to look more like his and satisfy every part of your soul. Don't give in to the desires of your flesh, but ask God to help you hold out until he shows you how he wants to fulfill those desires and his plan for you. Following *his* heart will leave you more alive and fulfilled than anything our own hearts could ever lead us to.

*Thank you, Lord, that you have the power to change my heart. I want to delight in who you are, and I ask that you will give me what my heart should desire. Thank you that you never leave me feeling empty. Bind my wandering heart to you.*

Journal

# Obedience

It takes obedience to discover all the Lord has for you and to truly walk with him. Obedience to God isn't something that you'll do one time only; it must be continual in your walk with him. Your obedience determines your future. God will ask you to do things that you don't understand, and he will ask you to go places that are out of your comfort zone. He will ask you to trust him beyond what you can see with your own sight. But the reward for obedience is beautiful. It's worth it.

I always think about "what ifs." Looking back on a decision, I think, *What if I hadn't decided to obey God? I wouldn't have what I have now, and I would be a completely different person.*

Often it is extremely difficult to follow the Lord in complete obedience. All I can see ahead looks like heartache, loss, and stepping into unknown territories. I pray that, if I have made the right decision, God will strengthen my faith to trust him. He has never failed me when I have acted in obedience.

Jesus' words sound loudly in my heart: "Blessed are those who hear the word of God and keep it!" (Luke 11:28 NKJV).

Right now, is the Lord nudging your heart to move forward in faith and obedience? It may seem like a scary time, and you know that moving forward in obedience will take a lot of trust. Ask the Lord to strengthen you to walk in confidence. Know that whenever you walk in obedience, you're stepping into something great that the Lord has for you. Satan hates that, and he will try to make you doubt. Keep going!

Once the Lord asked me to do something that was not easy, especially at that time in my life. Soon after I acted on what I knew God was telling me to do, doubts kept circulating in my mind: "Did God *really* tell you to do that? Are you sure you made the right decision?"

The next day at church, the sermon was about satan whispering to Eve in the garden, asking, "Did God *really* say you shouldn't eat the fruit of the tree of good and evil?"

Yep. That was God reassuring me that I had heard his voice correctly—and reminding me that satan's age-old mission is to try to get me to doubt God's voice.

## Day 19: *Obedience*

What if Jesus hadn't followed through with his obedience to his Father? What if he had failed to finish out his mission of going to the cross and dying for our sins? We would be without hope. Jesus knew the cost of obedience more than anyone. But he also knew the reward:

Have this mind among yourselves, which is yours in Christ Jesus, who, though he was in the form of God, did not count equality with God a thing to be grasped, but emptied himself, by taking the form of a servant, being born in the likeness of men. And being found in human from, he humbled himself by becoming obedient to the point of death, even death on a cross. Therefore God has exalted him and bestowed on him the name that is above every name, so that at the name of Jesus every knee should bow, in heaven and on earth and under the earth, and every tongue confess that Jesus Christ is Lord, to the glory of God the Father. (Philippians 2:5–11 ESV)

Jesus knew the end result: "*For the joy set before him* he endured the cross, scorning its shame, and sat down at the right hand of the throne of God" (Hebrews 12:2).

Chapter eleven of the book of Hebrews is known as the "Hall of Faith." Every single one of the people in this chapter was faced with a big decision. Would they obey what God was leading them to do? Or would they stay in the comfort of where they were? What if they had failed to obey?

Day 19 Challenge

I challenge you to go read the eleventh chapter of Hebrews. Don't turn a deaf ear to what the Lord is asking you to do. If he is asking you to do something that is extremely difficult, take courage that it will be worth it. He will carry you through and give you everything you need to do it. I challenge you to trust your heavenly Father, and to move forward in obedience.

*Thank you, Lord, that your plans are always good. Thank you that we can trust you when we walk in obedience to you. Thank you that the reward is so much greater than what we can imagine.*

Journal

# Race Day

When I was in middle school, I wanted to be a runner. I ran cross-country and track and trained all year round because I wanted to be good. I was pretty fast, and I loved it. Cross-country was a sport that my dad and I bonded over. My race was the two-mile, and we would talk all the time about strategies for how I was going to win. On race days he would pop out at certain points along the trail to yell my name and encourage me. I remember once seeing him in the woods somewhere along the race course, leaning against a tree and waiting for me to come running by so he could surprise me and tell me to keep running as fast as I could. He was definitely the only dad going to that extreme. It was great!

When we were running together, he would always say, "If you can make it to this point, you can make it to the next point. Find different target points along the way, and you will be able to keep going one at a time" (which is easier to say when you don't feel like you're going to pass out). I found that whenever my legs felt as though they were about to give out, I could fix my eyes on something ahead of me (say, a streetlight pole 200 yards ahead) and tell myself I could at least make it there. And then when I had made it, I could find another marker ahead to make it to. It was a way of breaking down an impossible task into smaller parts.

This idea can apply to more than cross-country running. Sometimes in life when you don't feel as if you can run any harder and you can barely breathe, you need to fix your eyes on a checkpoint. Then another. And another. Before you know it, the race will be over, and *you will have made it:*

> Therefore, since we are surrounded by such a great cloud of witnesses, let us throw off everything that hinders and the sin that so easily entangles. And let us run with perseverance the race marked out for us, fixing our eyes on Jesus, the pioneer and perfecter of faith. For the joy set before him he endured the cross, scorning its shame, and sat down at the right hand of the throne of God. (Hebrews 12:1–2)

I love that Paul compares our lives as Christians to running a race. It's a great analogy! Every time my team would show up for a cross-country race, the trail would be different.

## Day 20: **Race Day**

Some trails would be hilly and others would be flat and easier. Sometimes rain would be pouring down; sometimes it would be unbearably hot. In the race that we run as Christians, there are going to be many different kinds of courses as well. We will encounter different obstacles and various kinds of conditions. Some days our legs will be so heavy that we can hardly run, and some days we will feel as though we're flying.

Just like cross-country runners, we need to set checkpoints for ourselves along the "racecourse" of life. Sometimes the way is really hard, and halfway through you don't think you can make it anymore. Whatever you do, don't stop! You *will* finish the race. And the reward at the finish line is greater than anything you could possibly imagine.

We need perseverance. Notice how the verse uses the word *perseverance*: "Let us run with perseverance the race marked out for us, fixing our eyes on Jesus, the pioneer and perfecter of [our] faith."

Perseverance implies that your life will not always be easy, but if you have something in front of you to fix your eyes on, you'll keep going. What do you fix your eyes on?

Jesus.

Run toward him. He'll give you the strength you need to keep going. If you fix your eyes on him, you'll make it to whatever he has for you next. And then he'll be at the next checkpoint too!

# It's Worth It

The rest of the verse from Hebrews 12 reads, "For the joy set before him, he endured the cross, scorning its shame, and sat down at the right hand of the throne of God."

Jesus knew what was at the end of his race here on earth. He knew the reward. He knew he would sit at the right hand of God when it was all said and done. He kept his eyes *fixed* on the joy set before him, the joy of what was to come. Because of that, he could endure the cross: "Therefore, my dear brothers and sisters, stand firm. Let nothing move you. Always give yourselves fully to the work of the Lord, because you know that your labor in the Lord is not in vain" (1 Corinthians 15:58).

As a child of God, you have so much to do here on earth and so many treasures to lay up in heaven. Fix your eyes on Jesus. He's run the race before you. He knows every struggle, every hill, every rainy day, every beautiful day, every storm, and every muddy course there is to know. Run to him and ask him for the strength to *keep going*. You'll make it, because he'll give you everything you need to run the course:

> Consider it pure joy, my brothers and sisters, whenever you face trials of many kinds, because you know that the testing of your faith produces perseverance. Let perseverance finish its work so that you may be mature and complete, not lacking anything. (James 1:2–4)

## Day 20 Challenge

Keep running. Just as my dad ran out into the middle of the woods to find me on the cross-country trail and encourage me to keep going, Jesus is right in the middle of whatever situation you're in. No matter how hard or easy it is right now, he's there. Fix your eyes on him and run to him.

*God, thank you that you give me what I need at every check-point in life. Sometimes my legs get tired and I honestly don't know if I can run anymore. Life gets hard. But help me not to stop. I want to run, because I know it's worth it.*

Journal

# What's It Cost?

"I will not sacrifice to the LORD my God
burnt offerings that cost me nothing."

*2 Samuel 24:24*

After we finished filming *I'm Not Ashamed*, people asked me, "What is one of the biggest things you learned from Rachel's story, and what do you hope people take away from it?" Well, remember when I was asked about what my favorite scene to film? The answer to this question is similar.

About a year before I knew I would audition to play Rachel, God laid a message on my heart. A message of sacrifice. I was leading worship at a Wednesday night youth group and I got to speak to them about it. Little did I know the Lord was just scratching the surface of what he was preparing me for. It's incredible how he works.

## It's Worth It

When I was preparing this message, the Lord brought a specific passage of Scripture to my mind; it's in 2 Samuel 24.

To sum up what's going on here, the Lord told King David to build an altar to him on a certain man's land. The man was so honored that the king was at his house, and he offered King David everything and more that would be needed to make the sacrifice for free. Sounds pretty easy for David, right? David's reply sums up what the Lord had been teaching me: "No, I insist on paying you for it. I will not sacrifice to the LORD my God burnt offerings that cost me nothing" (v. 24).

It's moments like these when we see why God calls David a "man after my own heart" (Acts 13:22).

David resisted the idea of giving God something that didn't cost him anything. It wouldn't be a sacrifice if he did that. It would be cheap, and therefore it would mean nothing to God.

When you decided to follow Jesus, you were given some incredible things—hope, a purpose here on earth, and a beautiful inheritance waiting for you in heaven. But you also have to respond to something that Jesus asks you to do: "If anyone wishes to come after Me, he must deny himself, and take up his cross daily and follow Me. For whoever wishes to save his life will lose it, but whoever loses his life for My sake, he is the one who will save it" (Luke 9:23–24 NASB).

What does that mean?

We follow him, whatever the cost. We surrender everything to him, place it in his hands, and trust him. We change our drive for success, status, popularity, or money to a drive to follow Jesus. *Whatever the cost.*

Yet we all have a tendency to live the exact opposite way. We climb the ladder of success. We get in line first. We take what is ours, and we get to the top. These things are easy to strive for, but they always leave us devoid of purpose. They cause us to settle for a cheap substitute that will soon fade:

> Therefore, I urge you, brothers and sisters, in view of God's mercy, to offer your bodies as a living sacrifice, holy and pleasing to God—this is your true and proper worship. Do not conform to the pattern of this world, but be transformed by the renewing of your mind. Then you will be able to test and approve what God's will is—his good, pleasing, and perfect will. (Romans 12:1–2)

God asks us to do the same thing that David did. Back in Old Testament times, the people were required to sacrifice animals all the time in order to be cleansed of their sins. By the grace of God, Jesus became the ultimate sacrifice for human sin so nobody has to sacrifice animals on altars anymore. But in order to follow him, we have to take up our cross daily.

Remember the wording of the passage: "In *view* of God's *mercy*" offer your bodies as living sacrifices. Jesus was our greatest example. He lived a life fully surrendered to God; therefore, he was the most perfect sacrifice. His one desire and mission in life was to fulfill the will of God. By means of his death, he set us free from death. In *view* of that, we give our lives to God as living sacrifices.

But it does cost us something. Living sacrifices are dead to self.

Then we must turn to our further response: "Do not conform to the pattern of this world, but be transformed by the renewing of your mind. Then you will be able to test and approve what God's will is—his good, pleasing, and perfect will" (v. 2).

Paul explains:

You were taught, with regard to your former way of life, to put off your old self, which is being corrupted by your deceitful desires; to be made new in the attitude of your minds, and to put on the new self, created to be like God in true righteousness and holiness. (Ephesians 4:22–24)

## Day 21: **What's It Cost?**

In the same way, count yourselves dead to sin but
alive to God in Christ Jesus. (Romans 6:11)

We model our lives after Jesus. We pursue the glory
of God above all else. We daily surrender our struggles,
temptations, desires, and will. We put to death the cravings
of our flesh that rob of us living in our purpose. We consider others more than ourselves. We serve others, rather
than taking from them. We make ourselves last instead of
first. As a result, we don't resemble the world. We look
drastically different—as Jesus did.

Become a living sacrifice. That is the way to live in your
true purpose. Pick up your cross, and follow the Shepherd.
There will be times it will cost you—it cost Rachel Scott
her life. But her reward in heaven is so much greater than
anything of this world.

A living sacrifice is dead to self, but is fully *alive* in
Christ Jesus.

Will we offer God sacrifices that cost us nothing?

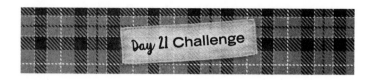

**Day 21 Challenge**

David refused to offer a cheap sacrifice to God. That told everything about his heart. I challenge you to become a living sacrifice. That's not cheap or easy, but it will show your devotion and love to the Lord. You will look drastically different from the world, but you will *shine*, and everyone around you will notice. Remember, it *will* cost you. It won't be easy—but the reward is so great. It's worth it!

*Thank you that there is freedom and life in following you. I don't want to offer you a sacrifice that doesn't cost me anything. That's not a sacrifice at all. In view of all that you have done for me, I choose to surrender my life to you, whatever it looks like.*

Journal

# About the Author

**Masey McLain** was born in Vidalia, Georgia, the third of four children born to Marty and Stephanie McLain. McLain grew up a pastor's daughter and attributes a lot of her love for the arts to her mom, who was a competitive dancer, singer, and choreographer. When McLain's family moved to Atlanta, Georgia, where her Dad would pastor a new church, Masey expressed to her parents her desire to become an actress, signed with a talent agency, and soon after booked her first commercial with Disney Channel where she had to sing for the Jonas Brothers.

Throughout high school, she continued to audition and book small guest roles in various TV series, as well as book principal commercial work. She landed her first lead role in a play when she was fifteen years old, where she won Most Outstanding Actress in her region's competition. McLain also started on the girl's basketball team at her high school as well as ran cross-country and track.

After high school, Masey went to college in the Atlanta area where she studied communications. With a musical background, she performed original songs in various coffeehouses throughout the Atlanta area and began regularly leading worship at her church. McLain made her first true mark in film when she played the lead role in her first feature film, *I'm Not Ashamed*. She continues to pursue an acting career while also communicating a message of passion and purpose to today's young people.

∞

You can send a message directly to Masey McLain via her official website:

## maseymclainofficial.com

She would like to know how this book, *It's Worth It*, or the film, *I'm Not Ashamed*, has made a difference in your life.

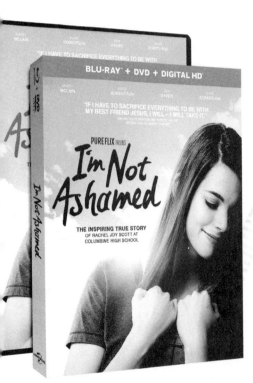